Atoms of Delight

IN THE MOMENT

Kenneth Steven

Saraband

Published by Saraband
3 Clairmont Gardens
Glasgow, G3 7LW
www.saraband.net

ISBN: 9781915089939

Printed and bound in Great Britain by Clays Ltd,
Elcograf S.p.A.

1 2 3 4 5 6 7 8 9

MIX
Paper | Supporting
responsible forestry
FSC® C018072
www.fsc.org

Contents

Contents

Introduction

I began thinking about this book by considering the idea of pilgrimage, and what the word actually means to me. The word is often used to describe the journey to a shrine or sanctuary in search of a spiritual transformation, which is a meaning I acknowledge. But now pilgrimage has become a much bigger thing for me; it has gone far beyond that rather heavy and medieval sense of going on a journey to visit a holy site. Why shouldn't it be about a walk to a hill loch to listen to the impossibly beautiful singing of red-throated divers? Why shouldn't it be about a child running into the forest in the early morning to find the treasure they dreamed of? These are journeys of the heart, seeking the profoundly precious places where little miracles happen. And why shouldn't it be about panentheism – the finding of God in all things?

Mine was a deeply religious childhood that stemmed mainly from my mother's own Free Church background, a Calvinist Presbyterian denomination found primarily in Highland Scotland. I feel pro-found sadness now for my mother, who grew up in a Highland glen beset by what must have been constant fears of transgression and damnation. She inherited those fears from parents who had known them all their lives: my grandparents were taught to believe they were 'not good enough', not suffi-ciently worthy to receive Holy Communion in their church. Yet both were devout members of their church in Glenurquhart, by Loch Ness.

I sat through many a Free Church service in the Highlands as a child, and almost invariably I'd emerge grief-stricken and terrified, certain that I too was on my way to perdition. Sundays – or Sabbath days as they were known – were a grim march through several services, composed of after-noons where I wasn't allowed to read anything but the Bible or a religious book of some kind. Other children had an even stricter time: one girl whose grandparents hailed from the Isle of Lewis saw black curtains being hung up on a Sunday, the Sabbath, in order to shut out the light – even on the most lovely summer day. Small wonder it often extinguished any sense at all of a loving God.

But then it was 'atoms of delight' I discov-ered in reading the work of the great twenti-eth-century writer Neil Gunn from Caithness, the north-easternmost county of mainland Scotland. It feels appropriate for me to want to occupy that same ground as Neil Gunn because his background was similar in so many ways. The community, and indeed the family in which he was raised, was steeped in a Highland Calvinist mindset. Gunn was liberated into an exploration of spirituality in which Zen Buddhism came to figure more and more prominently in his thinking and writing, yet there's a profound melding of those two worlds in his great work *Highland River*. The main protagonist in the end is on a pilgrimage of his own to discover the source of his childhood river. He imagines somehow that when he reaches that place he is destined to find something profound, something tangible and visible. The paradox is that there is nothing – or perhaps *everything* would be more accurate: there's the silence amid the wildscape of the Caithness Flow Country and all that inhabits it with such fragile beauty. But there is nothing Old Testament about the end of his journey: there is no great meeting and there is no returning with tablets of stone. What Gunn wants to communicate is important: since *Highland River* also carries strands of his own life, it's clear this is as much a reflection of his own spiritual journey from adolescence into adulthood.

At the same time, Neil Gunn pays tribute in the work to his parents and his wider community. There is no scornful disdain for their beliefs; instead, the father and mother are lovingly portrayed. This, after all, is the only world they have known, for they will not have travelled far beyond Caithness in their lifetime.

In *our* time we're witnessing the beautifully woven tapestry of our natural world fraying and tearing. At some point every day I find myself considering just what is being lost: climate chaos is all too apparent, but the relentless march of the extinction of species after species is there every bit as much, too. How we *respond* to that is complicated: already a kind of mental overload is widely acknowledged because so many individuals feel they can't cope with listening to the news.

Yet still it's better to light a candle than to curse the darkness. And that's at least in part what I seek to do here by sharing these pilgrimages. In going to a remote corner of the island of Iona to gather acorns that might perhaps have come from the descendants of oak trees planted by Columba's monks, I'm not doing anything of vast importance. And yet it feels healing just the same, the thought of bringing back acorns that then can be sent to others as little gifts, as future trees. Perhaps it's not such a little thing after all.

Introduction

Sometimes there doesn't need to be any great sense of message, either; sometimes it's enough to share a journey of celebration, of wonderment. I'd thought at some point of writing about the most amazing sledge run I've experienced in my life: I was with my great friend Dagfinn at the end of my first year in Norway and Dagfinn organised a sledge run for us. He himself was two metres tall and built like Tom Bombadil from *The Hobbit*. That sledge run lasted perhaps as much as a half hour; it took us down a long forestry track as the moonlight flickered through the trees and the freezing wind skimmed our faces. In the end I decided there wasn't enough to say, and yet I've told the story now just the same, and still it feels important. Important because of the weight of what we're carrying; the possibility sometimes of letting go and sledging again, to feel the wonder of the wind in our faces. No less and no more than that.

The sermons I heard in childhood left my faith battered and damaged but not lost. I think purely and simply because of my belief in a God who created an extraordinarily beautiful world – and not in some magical seven days – through evolution most certainly. The shreds of my own faith have an understanding and a profound love for the Celtic

Christian path. And that itself has been born from my growing understanding of the story of Iona, that small island off western Scotland known, indeed famed, for its natural beauty, its tranquillity, and the role of its Abbey in the development of Celtic Christianity – much of that together with my wife, Kristina. The Celtic Christian story and path are somewhat elusive, because there's a lot we don't know and are unlikely ever to discover fully about the beliefs and practices of those living in the early centuries in Ireland, Scotland and beyond. That can mean that, rather as with the New Age movement, an enthusiast can go off in pretty much any direction they like.

But there does remain more than enough that is known and plenty more that can be assumed. For one thing, it was about cherishing every strand of the created world. We know this through the stories the early Celts left behind; they reveal an important amount about the mindset.

For me the most profoundly beautiful of those stories is the one I first discovered in the work of Seamus Heaney, that of St Kevin and the Blackbird. Put in simple terms, the saint is on the shore in springtime; it's early morning as he goes down to pray. He stretches out his hands, and while he's far away in the world of praying, a mother blackbird spies the refuge of his hands and flies to them. He notices nothing, so embedded is he in the world of his prayer. And she makes of Kevin's hands her nest, laying her eggs there. When he 'wakens' from prayer he understands at once what has happened, but because of his profound love for all living things he can neither disturb her nor destroy the nest. When the other monks eventually come to find him, they understand his predicament. Over the next days they look after his needs, bringing him sustenance and keeping him warm. Then at last the fledglings hatch. The mother bird rises into the sky to offer a song of thanks to Kevin, for the great love that he has shown.

That's it for me; that's the parable for our time. If it's about anything it's about this, about learning at last to live gently on our earth and caring for it. Some of the pilgrimages I share here are ones I've known from earliest childhood, while others are ones begun or first experienced in adulthood. And there are a few too that remain to be made, promises I intend to keep. These pilgrimages are indeed about longings of the soul, but they're also about healing the soul, for several are about a true finding of solace. Whatever your own beliefs, these can be understood as pilgrimages equally well by those who do not have any faith in any deity, but who simply cherish our planet, nature and humankind, and who consider how to live well and responsibly as custodians of the Earth.

Vincent

See him now, swathing the southern fields;
ripe in the light and alive, hands
holding the whole circle of the sun, radiant
with the rippling of the breeze. What does he need
of a world lowering itself slowly
into the building of slums for children to cry in,
and factories where sadness
will be manufactured more exactly than before?
He is free to feel: his few years measured
by the way he sees what is beautiful,
and puts everything the world considers worthless
onto canvas for the rest of time.

Serpentine

My adult self stops at the gate at the end of the track that crosses Iona from east to west. I'm going to St Columba's Bay. It doesn't matter how wild the day is: actually I'm almost the happier for it being wild and wet, for then I'll have the chance to *coorie* deep into myself, to use the Scots word. When I make this walk, when I turn left at the gate and begin battling my way down to the bay at the island's south end, I feel I become a child again. We have so many labels. We carry them in our adult selves as mothers and fathers, as carers, as sisters and guardians and as however much else. And of course we need to and it's good that we do. But sometimes it matters too that we're back to being ourselves, that the labels and the responsibilities and the honours too, all the accolades we may receive, are blown out of us and we're back to who we really are, who we were to begin with, who always we were meant to be. It's akin to little scraps of paper being blown out of your pocket as you walk and battle against the wind. You feel small in that wind, truly small, and in a way you're blown back into childhood. It feels good and healing, to leave that adult self behind and be blown back into something deeper, something that might be more real.

For me I find it's the moment new words are born: not always, but often. Somewhere on that walk to St Columba's Bay I'll find a scrap of pencil and a notebook and capture the words that are pouring through my mind. Because it's as though I never wrote a single word before; I've been blown back into a place where it's all about starting again, about being new. And though that can happen at other times and in other places, it happens most often here, on the path down to St Columba's Bay and on the wildest of days.

What I find strange and almost eerie too is seeing my parents here; catching glimpses of them trudging on with bags and binoculars and whatever else. I see my younger self too, as excited as a puppy, running ahead and running back, exhausting myself in the process, because I've been yearning to get to St Columba's Bay for days and at last, at long last, it is happening.

Slowly they trudge up the last of the sandy path and onto the rocky track that leads up the last of the hill to the loch. However long ago they christened it the Khyber Pass and I remember still the small boulders being sore on my feet as I walked, as I scrabbled my way to the top. As I remember too being breathless by the time I got there and turned to see the islands of Tiree and Coll and Staffa and Rum, and even the misty perhaps of Skye somewhere beyond if we were lucky. But I didn't want to wait too long because I was aware of the danger of wasting time; there wasn't a moment to lose because soon we had to be down at the bay.

Now at last I was allowed to go on ahead alone and I needed no second telling. I was out on the path around the loch, then leap-frogging the boggy ground beyond it. Soon I'd be able to see it; soon it would be below me. I had to stop and be careful at the little notch, for there the descent is steep, but after that you're into the deep glen, and then I ran for all I was worth. I ran until I felt the wind about me, until I felt I might be flying, for it had happened and I was back.

The bay is held by rock arms. In the middle there's an arm too, so actually there's an east and a west part. It was here St Columba landed, that his curragh came in from Ireland in 563 AD. Into this bay not made of beautiful white Hebridean sand at all, but rather of rocks and stones. Nor is it any gentle sea lapping the lips of the bay; instead it's a bouncing of big waves, sometimes of waves so strong you'd be mad to go out too close. But now I'm there and crashing down the long beach over the boulders on that left hand edge of the bay, for that's where the treasure's found, and that's truly why I've yearned to return.

Somewhere out there in the deep waters between Iona and Tiree is a reef of serpentine. It's a soft rock and brittle. Sometimes bits of it must be broken off and rattled about by the big seas for however long before beautifully polished fragments wash in to the beaches of both islands. On Iona the best are brought here, to the bay where Columba landed. Indeed I always wonder if they knew, if he and his twelve followers came back here and found them too, these fragments of green stone – as though they carry in them a memory of Ireland. The truth is they were too busy surviving and building and journeying elsewhere; they had come to Iona with the urgency of the Gospel. This was no place for play.

There's a wonderful and extraordinary range to those green stones. Some are white pebbles with bright yellow or orange flecks. They look almost like sweets specifically designed to catch the eye of a child. Then there are the tiny St Columba's tears: pure and translucent fragments of serpentine small

as a pinkie nail. Theirs is a moss green, and sometimes I have to look at them long and hard to be
certain they're serpentine at all, for they might be
sea glass. In that case there's just something about
them that gives them away as artificial; a certain
'thinness' about their green. Last of all there are the
globes of pure serpentine, as large as a marble or
bigger still – or sometimes you might be fortunate
enough to find a translucent flake that fills half your
palm. And these can be anything from the colour
of pale grass to a deep jade, but there can be flecks
of blue and red too. The range of serpentine shades
never ceases to amaze me.

You're either a tide-dancer or a sifter. I had no
patience and I was the former; I was out always out
as close to the edge of the sea as I dared, watching
for any hint of green in the water or in the shingle. Of course sometimes it meant getting an ankle
soaked in freezing water, but if that meant grasping
a good green stone in the process it was worth it.
But I never risked going too far in my eagerness
for treasure; I learned to be wary of the sea here
and I've never forgotten that caution, even in adulthood. When you first see the strength of that sea
dragging back, when you hear the sound of it like
a long in-breath, you understand you have to be
careful. So I'll never get completely wet.

My mother was a sifter. When I'm back now I see her, sitting up on one of the mounds of shingle higher up the beach, patiently seraching the stones for pieces of green. It was she who first taught me to search, and I remember the first stone I found – at the age of four or five – indeed I have it yet.

But my father isn't here. You wouldn't find him crouching in the shingle looking for stones; he would have had neither the patience nor the interest. No, rather he's up somewhere on that middle spar of rock, hoping always for a great northern diver out in those bouncing waves, or perhaps even the pure beaten bar of a golden eagle that's floated over from Mull and is glistening up in skies that just sometimes catch an edge of sunlight.

He comes to join us in the cleft of rock where always there has to be a fire and tea. Already my mother and I are showing one another the stones we've found, planning where we'll go next to hunt. For the beach is big, perhaps as much as a hundred yards from its upper edge down to the sea. And the truth is green stones can be hiding anywhere, not just at the tide's edge or in the mounds of shingle lower down. I remember once being somewhere higher up the beach when it began to rain, great drops out of a clear sky. All at once I started seeing the different flecks of green; suddenly the white stones were turned dark and I went from one to the next, reaching for the newly revealed pieces of serpentine.

The truth is that the whole of the south-east corner of the island is studded with little secret coves where those flecks and pebbles of green are to be found. They have the most wonderful names too, all of them carried from the Gaelic, of course: the Port of the Young Lad's Rock, the Gully of Pat's Cow, the Port of Ivor's Cornfield, the Gully of the Chimney and the Port of the Small Streams. This is where I came in childhood, for it's easier for a child to clamber about here and find ways through and down to these coves. They're carved out of mighty walls of rock, and it might have been that once upon a time giants played chess here with great pieces of loose stone. Then they quarrelled and scattered the pieces from the rock board in fury. And the rewards for any treasure hunter are great, for few people seem to bother to search for green stones here. Or indeed for amber, and I have one little orange globe of it that turns purest gold when you hold it to the sun; I know that was found in one of those coves and I even know the name of the cove, but it'll die with me. I was told by the person that first gave me that morsel of amber it's the only place on Iona such stones can be found.

I think now if my parents had known just how rocky and remote these coves were they wouldn't have let me wander down here to find the little beaches they concealed. I liked them too because they were havens of cool on days it was hot and airless on Iona; the sun rarely if ever found its way here between these jagged spars of dark rock. I wonder if any of the great Scottish Colourist painters ever ventured here to capture the wind and the light on canvas. I can somehow imagine Cadell finding his way through the rubble of rock on a day the sky's bright one moment then all at once darkens, the waves below dappled and dancing.

I still come here, year on year, to be blown out of myself and back into childhood, and to find new words and green treasures. For in truth of all my pilgrimages this is the truest of them; they are as a path that hasn't wavered. And from them I carry back many things more precious than stones.

Stone

A little cave of green stone
smoothed by centuries of sea
to a pebble small as a pinkie nail,
chanced up out of the waves' reach.

Hold it to light and it changes,
becomes a globe of fractures;
a cavern of ledges and glinting –
not one green but many at once.

And suddenly I think of it bigger
as the whole of the human heart;
carrying the cuts of its journey,
brokenness letting in light.

The High Lochs

Half of me is Highland. My mother's people are from Wester and Easter Ross, on either side and to the north of Inverness. Many of them, if not most, would have been Gaelic speakers. I glimpsed the last traces of their older world in childhood, but now it seems akin to having peered through a gap between curtains into somewhere grey and misted. There were the last memories of my great grandmother who'd possessed the second sight; there were my grandfather's stories of strange sightings of creatures in Loch Ness.

I visited the edge of that world at Easter and during the summer holidays. Not only the homes of distant relatives; more often they were the croft-houses that belonged to my mother's childhood friends. Homes a thousand feet and more into the hills where I drank dark tea and listened to stories. From the age of four or five I remember hearing those stories and sensing their worth, stories often that had been handed down from past generations, stories that somehow were like raw, rough gems. They were to be kept safe; they were not for sale. They were an inheritance.

The world those crofthouses inhabited seemed almost composed of the same elements. Most often my father would drive a steep single track road to reach them. Usually it would be evening and the dark had set in, but if any light survived I sat in the back of the car looking out at the distant heather-coloured hills set against the smoky grey of the higher ones behind. A landscape with the shadows of dark and stunted trees. And sometimes I would catch the impossible blue shimmer of a lochan, for now and again we had reached that height.

So it is to me that somehow the lochans are like the people: rare things to be found in the high hills and sought after, never left too soon, listened to and then kept safe as memory, precious. Those lochs themselves were part of my childhood: summer pilgrimages, journeys and searches, whole experiences. I'm not sure how much evidence of them survives; I don't know if the old family albums still have pictures. Perhaps they do, but the main evidence of them lies buried in head and heart, in memory. I've always found the truth of that strange and yet wonderful, that memories of our truly special places, days and events can't be proved in any court of law.

The fossil imprints left in the mind can be chiselled out only as stories, because no other evidence survives. They're real, but proving their reality would be all but impossible.

My mother was a fly fisher. She'd grown up in Drumnadrochit, beside Loch Ness, though her parents had no connection to the place. They came from Wester and Eater Ross respectively: my grandmother very much from a Gaelic-speaking family. My mother had learned to fish from her father: he'd a boat on Loch Ness and though most of the stories have been lost, I know he caught several giant pike there. It's the kind of water where monsters most certainly grow, as the loch's obviously immensely deep and there's good feeding for fish. They face few enemies to this day: Loch Ness is never much fished.

What my mother sought to find as a fisher in my childhood and my years of growing up were the high lochs, and it was as much and even more because of the experience of being there that she sought them out. Long before the journey to discover one began, I remember the excitement of poring over the map with my mother and father, working out the best loch to find and the best route to reach it. My father had an instrument he used to measure the distance: carefully he trundled its wheel over the cloth of the map to work out how long the walk would take.

His maps were magnificent: ancient, ragged, cloth things that had to be handled and folded so carefully lest they fall apart. They were coloured most beautifully; the contours of the hills in brown and amethyst, rising to summits that were a smoky grey. There was a joy in going on journeys of the mind as a child; taking a single finger and tracing glens and rivers to their ends. More than anything I loved finding the most rugged places where the contours all but came together. I could imagine the ramparts of rock rising on either side.

I will never forget the climbs to find those hill lochs. In my memory they've melded into one. I don't remember ever following a real path, instead the climb (and always it was a climb, and sometimes a severe one) would be through heather. Even to a young child used to the outdoors, to running and exploring as much and as often as possible, those battles through heather were exhausting. Anyone who's attempted such a climb before will know that it becomes almost more like a kind of swimming. It's immensely tiring battling over tall clumps of heather often as tall or taller than yourself. I recall half-losing my balance many times, often having to stop as we climbed to gasp for breath. My father would be out ahead always; he was the hill climber and would have worked out the best way to find the loch. He was the encourager too, the one who'd call back to tell us we were making good progress, that there couldn't be much further to go.

The worst times were at the height of summer when the days were windless and there were horseflies to contend with. The heat seemed to rise from the dusty heather and the bracken, and breath felt hard to find, the air like warm wool. I've little doubt that many times there must have been adders around our feet, but mercifully our loud and awkward swim though the heather would have chased them off, for not once do I remember seeing a single one. Sometimes I felt like giving up, sure I could battle no further, and then at last I'd hear my father telling us he could see it; he was sure that he could see it. There was more crashing to be done by me before I saw anything, for I was a good bit smaller. But then I'd look up, my face wet with sweat, and my heart would sing for joy. I remember that moment now not a shred less clearly: the first glimpse of the hill loch. Set like a clear blue gem in the dun shades of the hills, there was the line of the loch. It always seemed an impossible blue, perhaps because it was set against such dark garments of moorland. Sometimes we had to change the direction of our battle through the heather because my father had taken us too far right or left. Doubtless I complained at having to go further still, but we set off again, crashing on through the great heather waves, sometimes so tall they'd swish dustily against my face.

And then we were there: we broke out from the sea of heather at last into the softer lip of land that held the loch. We would stand there, getting our breath back, happy and talking about this or that, even laughing now that the battle of the last half hour or however long was over. But what I remember then was an awareness of the silence. That silence seemed to come and meet us, and we began hearing again, hearing what I want to call the real world.

For that is what we had done; somehow we had risen above a world that didn't matter. Of course it mattered to the shopkeepers and the hotel owners and all those who had to be tied to deliveries and road journeys of whatever kind. But this was above all that and it was out of earshot of it all too. The silence flooded in to find us and suddenly we were quiet also, aware of the desire and the need to be quiet, perhaps because my father had heard the calling of a curlew, or because we were simply listening to the flickering of the breeze as it ruffled the surface of the lochan. The silence was like a thin and beautiful layer of ice, something you didn't want to break. And I looked about me, at all that lay around the lochan and up on the hillside that held it.

What comes to me is an awareness of a colour, the colour of those hillsides especially. It was a kind of amethyst, a dark amethyst. There would be small trees here and there, scattered among it: larches and rowans and birches. Junipers too, and sometimes gatherings of pines along one edge of the lochan. What I would look for right away was a beach, for a beach was ever the best source of wood: more than anything ancient gnarled pieces of bog-wood washed there and left however long before. What still amazes me to consider is that they were real beaches, strips of clear white sand made not of shells but of rocks broken down over however long. Those extraordinary white rims of beaches.

Now we knew our respective tasks. My mother had come to fish and she set up her rod, began working out where the best place might be to stand. Now I can hear the sizzling of the reel as she prepared it. Now I can see her fighting with the flies to attach them, especially if the breeze was strong. Now I can see her at the end of some promontory, casting and casting over the water. And I knew better than to talk, for I understood I was not to disturb either of them.

I can see my father too, his binoculars round his neck. And I'm aware this isn't the best time of day for him to be here. He has to make do with it, for it would be impossible to bring us here not long after dawn, or to keep us waiting until the dark had all but fallen. But those would be the best times to see birds. This is the worst time of the day, when the birds are roosting. He leaves the lochan and starts up onto one of the hillsides, listening and always listening. I can see him with his head to one side, listening. More than anything he wants to hear and see the most magnificent of all the moorland birds, the golden plover. But there might be the tell-tale coal black voice of a raven as it swims overhead; there might even be the bent gold bar of an eagle as it searches and searches the hillsides, relentless. Out on the water of the lochan too there could be divers: red or black throated, for that's where they have their nests, as far from that loud world below as ever possible.

My task was to gather wood and prepare a fire. I was never to light it, but everything had to be made ready for my mother and father coming back. Even in summer it could be cold up at a hill loch: sometimes we were a thousand feet and more high, and the chill came from the wind. As long as you kept moving it was all right and often you'd barely notice it. But crouch down on the white shore for a few minutes in the rocks and that cold began creeping into hands and face and feet. I would begin my search on the white shore, if there was one, because I was searching constantly for precious things.

I remember once finding garnets at a hill loch. They were worn down to tiny round red pebbles the size of a ball bearing, but I recognised them right away all the same. I had a few minutes on the shore hunting for treasure, and then I knew I had to start the search for wood. Sometimes I would be lucky and there would be several pieces of gnarled and ancient bogwood about me on the shore. More often I had to search for trees, somewhere beside the water or further out on the nearest bit of moorland.

There could be no breaking of living branches either; that would have been sacrilege. It had to be about finding old fallen pieces under a clump of trees or out in the heather. And there had to be some old grey heather too, for that was the best thing to start any fire. That went to the fire's heart, to the place the match must find first. What I had to make was a kind of broch, a construction composed of dry wood and heather that would take the kettle and make our tea.

Then they would come to join me, my father already with stories of what he had seen or hoped he had seen, and my mother most often with a single brown trout. Somewhere between one and two pounds, so slippery, and with that red-speckled pale belly. Beautiful things they were, and now as I sit here writing and remembering, I think of the smell they had. A watery earthiness. And if my mother had caught one fish, as usually she had, then already she'd be suffering guilt over killing it. I think it was the magnificence of the fish that struck her too, the knowledge that out of such dark water could be pulled this incredible wonder.

Then the reek of the fire, the smoke blowing everywhere, this thick blue-grey. And the thrill of sitting close to it, and warming your hands, because that cold was biting, even in July and August. At last the kettle boiling (and it had been my task to nurse the fire, to keep the dragon fed with dry heather roots and bigger bits of wood). The tea dark and scalding hot, the colour of peat. In my memory by then it would be perhaps five o'clock and already there was the realisation we would have to go soon. The day changing, beginning to age just a little, and sometimes the first spit of drizzle in the air.

There are two hill lochs in particular I remember, individual ones among the many down the long years. One must have been close to my mother's home glen, somewhere up in the hills a little to the west of it. I remember it partly because of the beauty of the Gaelic name: *Loch na Breac Dearg* – Loch of the Red Trout. But I remember it also because there my father saw a hawk he knew he had never seen anywhere else before. It too had red on it; a beautiful rust red. Later he even wrote a letter to the ornithological boffins somewhere in England, describing it and asking what it might have been.

But they offered no solution, either because they didn't know or else because they didn't want to give away the secret location of some rare species. He always suspected the latter was the case.

The second loch I remember specifically was with my half sister Helen. We had camped almost right under the ramparts of Suilven in Assynt, far out among those other dead dinosaurs of mountains set in the vast moorlands of Sutherland. In the morning we set out to walk back towards Lochinver, and the path took us close to a hill loch. I will never forget the wonder of hearing the song of the red-throated divers. Impossible to try to describe it, to tie it down with bare words. It's something only that can be carried, forever, somewhere in a place in the heart. It's what the great Highland writer Neil Gunn would have described as an 'atom of delight'. We carry those with us, those atoms of delight, perhaps eight or ten or however many of them we feel we've been given in a lifetime. I only know the song of those red-throated divers to be one of the most beautiful things I will know in all my life. And somehow it becomes the song of the high loch; the song of that place above and beyond the concrete struggle of our lives. It is the song of something ancient and precious. Something nothing less than a gift.

Journey

I have gone into a landscape
not to come back different
but more myself. It can take days
to go into the hills and listen.

Everything is miles of silence:
a stretch of loch so blue it can't be real;
an eagle floating in the sky –
at night the skies a breath of stars.

I leave behind my loudness
for a time; remember what it means
to swim again, to feel
way out of my depth.

Cloudberries

I'll never forget the first time I encountered cloud-berries. I was in Nordland, one of the four Arctic counties of Norway, together with a large herd of students. There were perhaps eighty of us in all: students, teachers and a handful of folk who'd guided us to this place in the high autumn hills. I had spent the night in a *lavvo*, a traditional Sami tent that's effectively a wigwam, and I'd shared it with two of the Sami students. Doubtless I would have driven them mad with all my questions about their world: I had still to understand what my Sami friend Lars once reminded me of much later, that the Sami have microwave ovens and mobile phones too. He said it gently, but made the point clearly enough.

This was much earlier, not longer after I had arrived in that Arctic Norwegian world for the first time. I had come here determined to find out what had happened to the Sami after Chernobyl, to know how much if anything of their old existence survived. I was still full of excitement; still pouring out question after question to try to understand their world more fully, to put together all the fragmented pieces of the jigsaw. Having hoped it would happen for so long it was the sheer thrill of the fact it was now happening. And then I went out of the *lavvo* that early morning, into the silence, and found cloudberries.

We were high up: I don't know for sure how high we really were and it doesn't truly matter. Nordland is a long sliver of a county where Norway is at its very thinnest. In fact from our college beside the small community of Rognan you could see the sea at the upper end of the fjord and in the other direction look at the mountains on the other side of the Swedish border. Norway's that thin.

I remember walking beyond; whatever else I remember I know I remember that. Because I'm not good with too many people at the best of times, and especially not in wildscape, in that kind of environment I love most deeply. The camp was rousing, folk from different tents talking and starting to come outside as I had done. I knew that before long we'd be getting ready to start the day in earnest and I wanted this time to myself. I wanted not just to look at it all but to experience it alone.

Cloudberries

So I started away from the voices, out deeper into the everything of it, until I couldn't hear the muffled voices any longer. And I stopped and looked and realised I was seeing cloudberries for the first time.

I wish now I had a photograph of it, or a painting. It's one of those moments when you want to freeze time and can't, because that's not how time works. All I can do now is go back and try to remember it as perfectly as I can. I was looking out over a landscape dotted with them, dotted with cloudberries. They stood out, even from far away, those points of vivid orange and almost white. The ground under them was wet and marshy, and I learned that day how much cloudberries love watery moorland. But what I'm missing out from the picture are the mosquitoes and the flies, for the sun is up now and there isn't so much as a breath of wind, and the air is loud with the *huzz* of insects. But I go running for my first cloudberry and bend to pick it. Before I do, I look at it and consider what it's like. Later on I decided to call them mountain brambles, especially for those to whom the word cloudberry meant little: the colour's wrong, but not the consistency. For they're made of beads, three or five or more, depending on the size of the individual berry. You notice the cloudberry's seed as soon as you taste it. That's the asp in paradise, though in all conscience it has never troubled me much. And the taste? It's a honeyed sweetness, a gorgeous burst of rich, soft loveliness. Tastes are notoriously hard to convey; we know them well enough, but describing them in words is difficult.

However high we were it was a landscape I recognised and loved because it was familiar to me. It was made of the same elements I had grown up with on autumn holidays to Rothiemurchus under the Cairngorm mountains. But this was a landscape that did not stop; it went on, and it kept on, and it went further still. Here, too, on this plateau that was however many hundred feet above sea level, there were cabins. They were dotted here and there across the moorland, the wooden cabins that Norwegians come out to at weekends for fishing, for hunting, for quiet. These days cabins are very different indeed; an oil-drenched and sophisticated society has installed every kind of luxury in them, but this was back before all that happened, and I'm glad I experienced them then.

My Sami friend Lars had a cabin that wasn't much more than two rooms: bare floorboards, simple bunks, a stove and a primitive kitchen, all sweet with the scent of pine. The whole point of the cabin was about leaving behind the busy world below and going up to find something different, something undisturbed. Those were the kind of cabins I saw about me that morning.

Cloudberries

The plateau wasn't just a bare back of rock and trees: it undulated – rose and dipped and rose again. There were hollows and little dark eyes of pools that I recognised as lochans. There'd be a sudden clump of birches, then nothing – bare moorland covered with heather and what I also recognised from Rothiemurchus as blaeberry. Then a clump of juniper perhaps and some bare rocks, and so the shadow of another pool. Another wide stretch of heather, breathed with amethyst now in autumn, until that flowed into a hillside and a few gnarled pines. On and on and on it went, into the distance of the early morning.

So for however long I darted from one cloud-berry to the next. I discovered they don't grow in clusters; you seldom if ever find a whole patch. Instead there's one here and one there in the spungy wetness of the moorland, and you're trying to focus on them alone as the flies find you again, as you rec-ognise the sound of a mosquito. Even now as I write this so many years later I remember the cloudberry world I went into. I've loved picking fruit, especially wild fruit, all my life; at one time I used to joke that if I wasn't able to write any more that's what I'd do. Back then I didn't know that the picking of cloudberries is particularly important to Sami men. At that bit of the autumn a few will go together and stay at a cabin, and all the following day and for however long they'll be out finding cloudberries, utterly content in that moorland wildscape. I encountered cloudberries again later in Norway in different places, and I went out looking for them, but this was the first time, and it lodged in a deep place in the heart.

Then I remember being back in Scotland, in my home county of Perthshire. I was with my mother and a good friend, and we were crossing a high part of Schiehallion, our local alp, that I've called always the magic mountain. This was a year or so after my time in Arctic Norway, and as so often I was missing it still.

They say the Arctic gets under your skin, doesn't ever truly leave you again. And then, suddenly, under my feet, as though a small miracle had happened, and wishful thinking had worked, there was a cloudberry. I sank to the ground to make sure: it was indeed one small and wizened cloudberry. It wouldn't have won much respect from the Sami men, but what mattered was that it was a cloudberry. I'd had no idea they were there, and what was important was that where one scrawny and shrivelled cloudberry was to be found there had to be others. So began the hunt for them that lasted however long.

Cloudberries

Schiehallion's a long spine of a mountain; a kind of tent. When you look at the tent from some places it's a pyramid, a sharp spine rising into the sky. But it's much duller from other locations, where all you see is the long back, the ridge. What I'm saying is, there's a great deal more to Schiehallion than might first meet the eye. All I know is I spent a long time looking for the treasure.

When I did stumble over them at last I realised they grew in good numbers. I knew by then too that there were patches of cloudberries elsewhere in Scotland – in the Cairngorms, not least, that part of Scotland that most resembles Arctic Norway. But I knew too there were plenty of other patches of cloudberry in Highland Perthshire, on others of the high hills around Schiehallion. I knew also from my reading that they'd been known and loved in the past. Back in the days when Highlanders went up to their shielings, to the high mountain pastures in the summer months, their hungry children would seek out the places they knew for cloudberries. I had learned the word in Gaelic and had found a hill in Perthshire that was named for its cloudberries. I'd discovered that at the excavated crannog sites on Loch Tay they'd found cloudberry seeds, so they knew the early people had gone looking for them and doubtless prized them even then.

Atoms of Delight

Once I found the cloudberries on Schiehallion and worked out pretty exactly when they ripened, I resolved to come back to collect them year on year. One of the first times I went with Kristina. I wanted this to be a high point in the year, a special place in it, a pilgrimage. It marked the start of autumn, the beginning of the days as they begin to rust. It's both an experience of a new year as it is a remembering, a journey back to the first time and place.

Norway

A waterfall in a horse's tail
whitens the lake. A field is ripe with sunlight.

Summer snow still lies
impossibly high. A child
with straw for hair
is learning to walk by falling

in a meadow made of reds and blues.
Her father is building a house

with bare hands,
singing something given him.

Conkers

I had a lonely childhood. I grew up in a big old house full of books and antique furniture. I was an only child and I loved my own company, spending hours and days far away in my imagination. I remember when the wife of my father's uncle died. She had spent the last years of her life as a miser. Though left with a fortune by her husband who had passed away years before, she chose to live with bare light bulbs in sockets, sitting by the single bar of a simple electric heater. Her husband had been a ship's captain, sailing tea clippers to and from India.

All I'm left with now are the shreds of the story that surrounded him, for there's no one alive from whom I can find out more. But I know that he spent time ashore in India and, during his explorations, acquired a great many things he brought back with him. The most exciting my father told me of was a large uncut emerald given to him by an Indian prince. When his wife ended her days in some large and lonely house, all her belongings came to our home, as my father had been appointed executor of her estate. Perhaps half a dozen trunks were brought up to our attic, in addition to whatever else that came to the house. I was five or six. I can still remember the utter joy of being able to go through those trunks, to ransack them. It was as though I had been washed up on some treasure island, and with me was the cargo of a pirate ship. I will never forget the thrill brought by those days. There were silks; there were medals; there were objects made of old leather that possessed a smell I can remember yet. It was as though I entered a whole story book and went back down some magic corridor in time. I'm not sure now I can say how long I was there, as it were. But for the first time in my life (for it has happened on however many other occasions since) I felt truly out of time. By that I mean that time no longer mattered anymore, almost no longer existed. Long afterwards, I'm still somehow not sure if it was several hours or many days. What matters is that I was there and that it happened. I am reminded, as I observed at the high lochs, that we are given perhaps half a dozen such moments, these atoms of delight, in our lives, to be treasured like pearls on a string. They're ours and ours alone.

But I wasn't given the emerald. That went to a relative my father felt had missed out otherwise. It didn't matter how much I wheedled, I was not going to get it. I remember it still, that great uncut stone in my small hand. It was huge: at least to a five or six year old child it was. But it was destined for a different home. What it did give me, I believe now, is my life-long love of gemstones. I became a kind of Gollum, fascinated by raw gems and faceted ones alike, holding them in the light, simply watching them.

We left that first house in Helensburgh not long after and came to Perthshire, to Crieff at the heart of inland Scotland. It was an old-fashioned town then. To begin with my parents couldn't find a house and lived in a tiny end of terrace place in the lower part of Crieff. I remember only the greys of it now and the greys of lower Crieff – the poverty of it. I remember derelict buildings and rather ghostly streets, a grey sadness over all of it. I'll never forget visiting the old shoemaker close to the high street and the greyness of his workshop. My mother had to persuade him to take sufficient money for the mending he had done to my shoes in the strangest kind of reverse haggling. He was the kindest and most generous of men; it's hard almost to imagine such kindness and generosity in a new time, where money has come to rule.

In Helensburgh I'd been in a sheltered little prep school with perhaps fifty other children – if there were even that many. Now I was plunged into the horrors of Morrison's Academy where there were well over a thousand and where sport mattered far more than anything else. I was desperately short-sighted and desperately shy and after however many days or weeks I began to be eaten alive by the bullies – and no-one did or said anything about bullying in those days. Well, actually they did. My parents were called in to explain the bullying, and they had to apologise for me because I wasn't standing up for myself. The physical bullying I experienced at Morrison's Academy went on for however many years on a daily basis. I can only describe that existence as a climate of utter fear. But I survived, and not everyone did. I have a friend from my class who didn't. He lives in London now, carrying the scars of those years of physical bullying and torment yet. He always will.

I survived, I think now, by going into some very deep place inside. I knew great love both from my mother and my father, and their love meant a vast amount. Yet somehow even that wasn't sufficient. For a long time they didn't know how bad the bullying really was, and I didn't tell them because I feared I'd be letting them down. I knew they struggled to find the fees to send me to a private school and I was afraid of failing their expectations. So for a long time I seemed almost to inhabit a cave which even the bullies could not reach. It was the absolute inner core of myself, and I know that that's the place too where I first found a pen. It's where my imagination truly came alive and where I started to write, at the end of my days in primary school and during the first of those secondary school years, when the bullying was at its very worst. I know for sure the two things are linked.

The autumn has been my favourite season always. When the wind comes back to the trees. When the rowanberries hang in orange clusters and the fields turn ripe and golden. When the rivers are wild again and the rain is coming in gusts against the windows. When the geese return in straggling skeins from Iceland and the open fires can be lit. When the chestnuts are huge and spiky on the trees, the hands of the leaves on their trees turned that wonderful burnt orange.

Like all the boys I kept a close eye on the horse chestnut trees to see how the conkers were developing. In those days all the children did. Getting a hoard in October was important, and everyone knew the trees that really mattered. There was one above where we lived in Crieff, under the main hill that was called the Knock, and that was the one that was ever in my sights. But not only in mine: there would have been any number of other children who knew that tree, who watched and waited for just the right time.

I feel now that those were the first pilgrimages I made, to the chestnut tree. I know they happened many times, over however many years. I don't think I was always successful; at least once I would have got there to find only broken shells and no treasure. But that's not what matters now; what matters instead are the nights lying in bed at the top of the house, listening to the wind howling about us.

I remember believing that somehow the house had roots and that they were being shaken. I remember going to the window, looking out from behind the curtains to see the moon being blown through the clouds – or so it seemed.

I can remember getting up at what seemed like the middle of the night to go outside. Most likely it wasn't then at all but perhaps rather somewhere between five and six in the morning. I couldn't go back to sleep, because I was thinking about the wind in those chestnuts. I got dressed without a sound and crept downstairs (I knew where every creak was hidden). In the porch I pulled on my boots and a jacket, then I was out into the full power of the wind.

I can remember what it was like to be blown uphill, as though somehow on the back of a horse. The thrill of that feeling, and of being hurried by the wind. The ghostly grey of the sleeping streets where we lived as I ran higher towards the beginning of the Knock and the woods that robed its sides. After going through gates there was a place where you climbed over a fence and into the field where the tree stood. I can see it now in my mind's eye as I write, and feel again that surge of joy at the knowledge I was nearly there. There was always a horse in that field but I worried for not a moment about any horse; a dragon couldn't have kept me from that tree now. It stood over on the far side of the field and beyond it was a house. It was more important I did nothing to waken that house.

I went across the field like a ghost, the wind still coming from everywhere and roaring through all the woods. I believe it's then I saw and understood for the first time how the wind isn't in one place at once. I would look down on the trees below the Knock and see the wind in one patch of trees but not everywhere. It seemed strange and wonderful at the same time. I ran until I was underneath the tree and almost always there would be the most tremendous sense of relief, for there were any number of whole conkers; green and spiky helmets on the brown earth under the branches. In those first few seconds I would try to gather everything at once as though I might be robbed. I reached out left and right, piling the treasure high in my gathered arms, and bit by bit I would grow calmer. There was no one else in the field – I had got here first after all.

Nobody could take this away from me now. I started instead to look for the best of them, to leave the rest behind. It was the indescribable delight of breaking open the biggest of them to find those sleeping giants inside. The sheen of them when first they're revealed, the smell of them. That deep and woody smell.

And all the time any number of others falling around me as the wind came gusting. They thudded into the muddy ground and I went running to find them, one after another until the shadow of school found me and I knew I had to go.

Truly the sum of the parts doesn't equal the whole. I was given so much more than a white bag of polished chestnuts that looked as though they were made of the same leather that the old shoemaker had worked with and restored. I felt given a whole world. It was about the autumn and the big winds, about the thrill of running up that long hill and entering the field at last at what felt like the middle of the night. It was about being there again another year and knowing I was the first to get there, that all this treasure was mine. It was about being in the wild world and feeling alive in it, truly set free to seek and to find. It was about all of that and more, and that was the start of the journey.

Autumn

I opened the door into the wood and listened:
through the low wool of the mist
the last leaves dwindled like dancers
down to a golden floor.

It was me that broke the silence:
my boots splintered a single twig
so the whole wood shook and rattled with wings;
the roe deer froze, their eyes all glazed.

Everything listened then –
the silence a waiting, the quiet a watching;
until my feet had disappeared, my shadow
    passed,
and only the rain fell still in soft glass beads.

The Pool

I've never liked the summer. I dread it even more in adulthood now that climate change has drawn out and made our summers hotter, even here in Scotland. But back then in childhood it was for other reasons that dread was there. For one thing, I suffered asthma all through my early years. I remember all too clearly those endless nights when I struggled for every breath. I grew up in dusty old houses filled with antique furniture and ancient carpets – even now I can see the dust rising in the rooms. I loved the dark wood and the hiding places those crumbling houses offered – the secrecy and somehow the magic of them – but I know now they hardly did me much good. And they were worst of all in summer.

By the time I was in Perthshire and into secondary school summer meant holidays all the same, and like every other child the prospect of long weeks away from school thrilled me. For me that freedom was even more pronounced because it meant escape from the unrelenting misery of bullying. All our summers started with weeks on the west coast or in the

Hebrides: if not Iona then Coll or Colonsay, Barra or Harris. Those weeks gave me the most incredible bond to the wildscape of the west. They took me from the inland, the only truly landlocked part of Scotland, to the freedom of the beaches and the sea, to caves and the hope of otters, water lilies and the secret shores of hill lochs. There in the west I was free range, my parents fearing no more than barbed wire and strong tides. I remember being out of the holiday cottage in whatever place we were staying and down to the shore at five in the morning. The front door was never locked and that was a metaphor for our days in the west. This was a different world.

But when we came back to Perthshire the weather changed. It was July. The days were heavy and overcast and muffled with thunder. Everything was overgrown and felt strange. I hung about the house and didn't have enough to do, and my parents got tired of me being under their feet. I was sent out to pick fruit.

I knew where my parents would send me. The farmer who owned and ran the farm was a burly man, somehow reminiscent of a bullock, with a straw mop of hair and fiery eyes. He lumbered about the place, peering over at what we were doing, shouting at those who were shirking and telling us we had to get a shift on, that we had to finish a certain field before we moved to a new one before lunch.

The Pool

Ordinarily I loved picking fruit. I would go into what in Scots is called a *dwam*, which takes any number of English words to explain. A dwam is your own world; an inner world where you're deep in your own thoughts, only dimly aware of what you're doing and what's going on around you. But that was with *wild* fruit. I was hardly in a dwam when picking fruit on a farm. In truth it was all a bit too reminiscent of school.

I picked well enough, and was happy to pick for long hours at my own pace, content when left alone. I would put up a short protest at home about going to the fruit farm, but deep down I knew there wasn't a chance of winning this one, and that for the next few weeks my fate was sealed. I sighed heavily, aware already I'd be up at seven the next morning.

We were picked up in an old van in the town square and I would crouch deep in the shadows, wanting to be out of sight as the others chattered and laughed on the van's floor in the blue stink of the exhaust fumes. A dozen of us might be crammed inside in the end, until finally we were there and let out at the bottom of the long dusty track below the farm.

The next hours I would work as fast as possible, hoping the bull of a farmer had left the field for a time at least. Except when he did the raspberries started flying as boys and girls threw them from behind their rows in a fruit war that went on until the bellowing was back and he'd returned to restore order. I remember days when thunder would grumble round us and the hours were sticky and hot and airless. The low cloud never lifted but hung down low over trees and river. I loved it when it did rain: the cool of the big drops falling on hot hands and arms. Sometimes an edge of cloud lifted and a molten sun poured through for a time, coppery and stifling. The river itself silted over the stones somewhere in the trees, low after weeks of little rain. It was not a true river now but the ghost of one: a slow and sultry reluctance flowing sullenly towards the sea.

I felt dusty and listless and only wanted away from those fields and this long labour in the heat. But I didn't truly know where I wanted to be instead, except perhaps back somewhere by the sea, exploring all on my own, searching for sea urchins and hoping always for otters.

Then, one day, we went to find the pool, a few of us. That in itself is strange because I seldom had much to do with the others. I don't quite remember how it happened; most of that is muffled now, wrapped in the wool of those hot and clammy days. I only remember fragments, pieces of the magic it was. I'm not sure exactly where it was nor how we got there – only of the joy of what it became.

The Pool

It must have been after a day of picking. The place was close by, perhaps half a mile off, and we'd have got there by farm tracks, for that whole belt of country was linked by them. It was all sheep farms and gates and tracks; a veritable warren of them that was difficult to negotiate, to find your way about with any accuracy. But the others would have known better than me, as this was where they'd grown up. I knew bits and pieces of it from exploring with my father in the hope of a cuckoo or some other treasured bird. He was a passionate ornithologist, and that meant getting up at some ungodly hour to go out skulking along riverbanks. I therefore knew it in a vague and unlinked way, but not at all well.

I do remember getting to the woods and going into them, and that in itself was a delicious thrill. Because for so many days we'd been out in the open fields, not in the full sunlight but beneath the muffledness of its thundery, metallic, beating heaviness just the same. Suddenly we were under the canopy of the trees and I remember the flickering light that passed through them and moved over the woody dark green beneath. We went together, slow and steady, deeper into the trees, towards the rush of the river.

And now the laughter and the fooling and the stupidity was gone, they were quiet. For there it was – or what was left of it – silver pathways that found their way among tree roots and flowed down into the deeper darkness of pools the colour of smoky quartz. Then higher at last we caught a glimpse of it: a single horse's tail of water coming down from the hills in a fall that was thirty feet and more tall, landing in a broad pool however many feet deep. We ran towards it, knowing we'd reached our goal.

None of us had swimming things. We cared not a fig about being naked. In fact, that was all the better after the long string of dusty days. There was a loveliness in the feel of the water; the cool touch of it against the skin. There is something magical about being held by water, about the deliciousness of that gasp of cold when first you're under and it's hugging you. I remember bobbing that day, for the pool was far deeper than we were tall, and sometimes you'd drift under some of the fall, and the force of it was almost sore for a moment. Then you'd emerge and lie on your back, looking up through the patterning of the leaves at that strange grey sky behind. The fruit farm, the farmer and even school were washed away at last. Nothing but the magic of this remained. At that moment I wanted it to last forever, but in fact it happened only once, and all I can do now is re-enter the memory; even the name of the place is gone. But this is enough: it was a gift, and through words I can re-enter the water of the pool, and all the wonder it brings.

The Pool

Coll

I got up long before dawn;
opened an unlocked door
into a landscape made of moor and loch.
Twelve years old: the only danger barbed wire
fences.
I ran until the hillside turned to sand,
and under me the whole Atlantic
softening the white rim of the island
like a sigh. I chased down all the dunes,
barefooting sand so white it might have been
a kind of snow. Sea breathed
in ledges and descents, in many blues
that melded into one. I dared undress
to tread out deep until I lifted
held and unafraid, breath
caught and stolen by the cold.
I entered another world;
melted into something else.
I came out strange and shining, new
and wandered slowly home, the same
yet never quite the same again.

A Treasure

My father had grown up with an obsession for ornithology. He told me how it had come about, too. So often we think of the questions we should have asked, the things we should have talked about before we realise it's too late – but this was something he did tell me in time. My father and his two brothers had grown up in Helensburgh and back then, not all that long after the end of the First World War, the town was still surrounded by what I like to describe as wildscape. My father's elder brother Douglas suffered from chronic asthma that would take his life in the end. All the same, despite the breathlessness that must have afflicted him day after day, he introduced my father to ornithology. He took him out into the country that surrounded the town just half an hour from Glasgow and taught him birds: how to recognise their flight, their songs, their nests, their eggs. And back then there must have been the most remarkable birdlife around Helensburgh to encounter: evidently, as during the summer months the brothers used to throw stones to scare away the corncrakes that were making such a racket in the fields through the night.

By the time I was experiencing my first years in Helensburgh too it had perhaps doubled in size, and most of that wildscape around it was little more than a fading memory. Then we moved as a family to Highland Perthshire, and my father's game became to try to see a hundred different species of bird each month of May. He was still writing articles for various magazines in Scotland, so often enough the stories of what he had seen and encountered in wildscape would find its way into the pages of his features. There would be trips to St Andrews because there he could encounter the coastal birds we had none of in our landlocked bit of the glens. There would be at least one climb to three thousand feet for the chance of glimpsing ravens, eagles and the magnificent black and red throated divers in their high lochs.

But all of this began on the first of May. That was when the list began; that was somehow the pushing out of the boat. He might see thirty or more different birds on that first day of the month, so it meant getting up very early in the morning, the whole family in tow. Very early in the morning meant half past five or six, when the birds were stirring and active. My father seldom if ever bothered about birdwatching by the time most bipeds were up and about and busy. It was early morning and early evening that mattered. So whatever the weather we were out before dawn on the morning of the first of May.

There was another birdwatcher with whom my father competed quite seriously during the years we lived in Crieff. This friend was taken by the thought of making a May list, of reaching a hundred by the end of the month. The difficulty was that the rules of the game were slightly different for each of them. For example, it was quite all right for him to *hear* a bird; for my father that bird could only be counted if he had *seen* it. I can still remember my father becoming truly cross – a thing that happened seldom enough – because his rival had heard a tawny owl from his bath and was insisting on counting it.

I can't ask him now how he decided which place he'd choose for that first day, for the start of a new month of the challenge. Sometimes it would be down by the river Earn, padding along the paths long before the dog walkers came out. Sometimes it would be up at Glenturret where there was ever the chance of a cuckoo or a green woodpecker in the higher woods and hills. But what I remember more than anything else is that morning in Aberfeldy.

For whatever reason I had gone alone with my father. I was slightly older now, perhaps thirteen or fourteen, and though I hadn't descended into the grey tunnel of gloom and grump, I still wasn't fond of early mornings. Consequently I can't even remember now how my father managed to rouse me, or get me outside by half past six. I have no memory of breakfast; no idea how I got into the car or precisely where we went. All I have is a very vague memory now of where we ended up walking; I was two or three paces behind my father, looking daggers at his back, saying not a word and sunk in the mire of misery.

It wasn't all that unlike the place where we were walking. It couldn't have been far from the Tay, except that this had nothing of the open loveliness of the river, for I knew those stretches well enough. I'd explored its beaches where sometimes I'd be lucky enough to find a pearl mussel shell or see the flimsy nest of some bird or other in late April or May. The Tay was open and wide and full of light: everything that this place was not at whatever ungodly hour of the morning.

It was a dark and smelly corridor through which a barely visible bit of water seeped. There were thorns and branches to avoid constantly so I was hunched forwards, trying to avoid being jabbed in the eyes and trying also not to stand on pieces of wood that might snap, ruining any chance of seeing a bird. In that moment, though, I frankly wasn't bothered whether we saw a marsh harrier or a blue-eyed bunting; all I wanted was to be back home in bed and sleeping.

And it was then it happened. It's at exactly such moments when you feel things couldn't become much worse that you're given something that changes everything, and, just now and then, for-ever. For down that stinking little slither of water, through the tangle of branches and brambles, came a single living jewel of luminescent blue and green. It came fast, low to the water, and somewhere I caught red on it too – in fact orange rather than red – and I held my breath as my father and I stood there, stock still on the path or what passed for one. I knew without him having to tell me that we'd wit-nessed one of the kings of birds, the great treasure of the rivers – the kingfisher.

I've never seen another in my life. I learned later that they're rare in Scotland, and almost not present at all in Perthshire. In the past they were the victim of harsh winters, though now that such winters are all but lost to climate change it may be that they're faring better. Still, I've only ever seen that one, and it's as though I keep the memory of that morning in a special box in the attic: like something you're given as a child that you take out only sometimes to show others, because you know how awed they'll be and how their response will burnish your own sense of wonder each time, too.

Even so, I don't go out birdwatching at half past five in the morning on the first of May. What I do is wake up and remember, go there again in my mind. Perhaps if I had the chance I would take my child, Willow, to experience something of what it all meant. But the truth is I didn't inherit or learn the skills my father was given. I didn't know how to go into a wood and stand in absolute quiet and be able to distinguish one song from another. I didn't go with my father into the high hills to see the shadows of birds on lochs and know for certain what they were. I'm all too aware I didn't ask enough questions. As almost all of us feel at some point or other in our lives, I didn't fully see what I had to inherit before it was too late and taken away. All I have are the boxes in the attics, with the kingfisher and the curlew and the golden plover and however many others. When I open those boxes I'm given whole days again and places, not just the sighting of a bird. Those are the boxes I open each first of May, to go back down those long tunnels to find my father, and to return to places and days long gone. They're different kinds of pilgrimages but they're real enough all the same and they matter, they count. And some day I'll give those boxes to my child.

May

Mossy pigeon voices in the trees;
the pond all sunk and silent, the lilies wide —
their open yellow eyes,
the whole long drawn-out daylight of the day.

A strange moon hoisted then at last
and hanging low above the hill —
a ball of cobwebs in the just blue sky;
a sky that will not quite get dark.

As down below the river slips to find the sea;
the flickering whisper that is left of it —
no breath of wind, the bats going back and
    forth —
in endless shadow-play, in mime.

Agates

I don't remember when I first met them, nor how or why we were in touch from the beginning. But whatever the connection, we soon got on to agates. Scotland is blessed with many gemstones. By that I don't mean the important, truly sparkling ones like emeralds or diamonds. There do happen to be some of the precious gems in remote corners, but they're gnarled and worn things, ground down by glaciers and long millennia at the top of mountains or the edges of rusted volcanoes. No, I mean semi-precious stones: amethyst and smoky quartz and carnelia. Agates.

Fife and Angus are full of agates. I learned that once I'd met Robin and Jean, and joined them on many an expedition hunting them. To me, they're pilgrimages now: those times themselves have gone into the ground and become a layer of something I can dig out with the pen. When I recover them I can hear whole conversations again and I'm back with them in strange nowhere places I could never hope to find on any map. I can remember going with them to visit some of their friends on the south side of the Tay, down at the bottom of strange hillsides where they said there was a microclimate that allowed them to grow things that couldn't have grown elsewhere. They had a tiny cat that had lost part of its tail: a buzzard had once flown down and tried to carry it off and like Tam O'Shanter's mare it had lost half its tail, but also the courage to go outside. That's only one story. I was given far more than just agates.

But let me return to the stones, for the word 'agate' will be unfamiliar to some. It's easiest to compare them to cut trees with their rings. The bigger they are, the more rings they'll have. But an agate possesses something more: colour. Sometimes at fairs I'll see cheap agates for sale, dyed with lurid pinks and blues and greens. The real colour that surrounds the rings, at least in Scotland, is often a beautiful grey – just as you see in the blue-grey sheen of a cat's smoky fur. But the Fife and Angus agates take on the shades you see in the pantiles of the roofs, that wonderful sandy-red.

I'm not sure how agates are born, so to speak: all I know is that they are, and that Scotland – especially those east coast counties – is blessed with some of the finest in the world. Every spring Robin and Jean used to drive back to their north of England home with a full ton of stones in the boot of the car. But there had to be a hunt for every single one.

You can find little fragments of agate on the shores around Montrose: you might be fortunate enough to stumble on something bigger and finer close to Scurdie Ness lighthouse if you're willing to spend sufficient time looking. But the real agates lie sleeping hidden in the fields inland, undiscovered.

There are rules to the game. Every winter Robin and Jean would be in touch with farmers in both counties who had become friends after years of treasure hunts. I can remember asking them what the farmers made of these visits and this hunting, and I still recall Robin's affable smile at the question: he was a gracious and gentle man with a twinkle of humour at the edge of his smile. He said most were bemused by it all; they neither objected nor cared much. Only when the couple visited the farmhouse (for they went to every one) with a cut and polished slab of agate from their own fields as a gift did they think again about those strange lumps of stone lying buried beneath their feet.

Here's a typical day. I would meet them from my home in Perthshire at the railway station in Dundee. Typically it would be a windy and wet morning in late March or early April, the cold so bad it hurt your hands and face. The back of their small van would be filled with everthing: old raincoats and boots, boxes and newspapers. Somehow I knew that their Yorkshire home would be little different. Once I had got in I was to shove it all out of the way. Either we'd drive out over the Tay Bridge into Fife or else east from Dundee into Angus. I can remember one disastrous occasion when I was told I was to navigate (Jean wasn't really the type to suggest first). I got my directions wrong and wasn't asked to navigate again.

With a mixture of map-reading and luck we ended up all the same at farms with wonderful names (Fife in particular is blessed with them: many, to my ear, that Tolkien might have conjured). Tinkler's Hill or Windy Gully or Black Boar's Ridge: these are half-invented, but the sounds intend to convey something of the real names. What I liked so much when I arrived at these farms was that I didn't truly know where I was anymore. I was off the map, somehow out of reach. No-one ever came out of a farmhouse to meet us; I was glad of that for I'm ever fearful of what Gavin Maxwell called a waterfall of dogs. No, the three of us would just sit in the car to be out of the wind and the rain and drag on jackets and waterproof trousers and finally our boots. Then it was out into all the weather threw at us.

Agates

I've often thought afterwards that our attitide to
what we're doing is so defined by the end result. In
childhood each autumn, in what still were called the
tattie holidays, I was made to go off each morning to
visit some farm and spend the day bent double gathering baskets of potatoes. I came back in the evening as miserable as a Free Presbyterian minister on
a sunny Sabbath. Because I was gathering only cold
hard lumps of potatoes that hurt the hands in the
end, it felt somehow pointless. Yet here in a field in
Fife or Angus I was doing almost the same thing at
the other end of the year and loved every moment.
The farmer had ploughed the field: that was central
to everything as the hunt for agates could happen
only if the ploughing had just been done. And it mattered we could hunt a few days after that ploughing,
otherwise the sleet and rain of early spring would
have washed the soil into a mush where little could
be seen. More than anything, the stones had to be
visible, for you need to learn to recognise an agate.

So it was that the three of us walked up and down
the lines of the ploughed field, our heads bent to
check every stone we passed. Usually it was a day
that was somewhere between snow and rain, and
that's the worst cold there can be. One thinks of
the men in the trenches in the springs of northern
France and imagines conditions like that – and we

were just playing. I can remember being in fields on the edges of hills, some of them with tight lines of pine trees.

As I write now I remember climbing one of those hills: the ground under me full of that Fife redness, and the sky above pure blue as for a brief time the armies of clouds passed and it was cold only, freezing cold, yet the sun blowing over us a daffodil light. But while I saw all that for a second I was still searching the ground below, and paradoxically enough for stones about the same size as potatoes. Often it was the very nobbliness of them that made them agates, as they have a kind of reptile skin you get to learn and recognise, with strange bubbles and lumps on the outside that give them away. That's why you don't want the rain to have encased them in mud because then that skin is invisible. So I'd stagger along the rows, bent double and freezing, yet loving every moment because I knew I was hunting for treasure.

These potatoes, of course, need to be opened. The truly exciting thing about every agate is that you have no idea what it'll be like until it's sliced – cut like a tree so you can see the rings and the colour inside. Some agates are beguiling; they have nobbles and that classic reptile skin on the outside, yet when the diamond saw has been taken to them to halve them, to slice them, there's nothing but greyness inside. Others that you pick up and carry with you anyway, that don't look as though they are going to hold much promise, open to reveal rings and colour you can scarcely believe. Go to the internet to find pictures of some of the celebrated agates from Angus and Fife: each is unique and all are breathtaking. Somehow they make me think of the Northern Lights, of those haunting flames rising into the night sky.

But none of that was revealed in those fields at the end of March. All I did was entrust those grubby potatoes to Robin and Jean, and wait patiently for long weeks until Robin had had time to open my box of treasures, to polish the cut faces of each stone and send them back to Scotland. I was like a five year old when I lifted the lid from that box with trembling hands. The best of those agates stands on a shelf in a window now, and I remember the exact moment I found it.

We had finished for the day and were leaving the field where we'd been gathering agates for however many hours. And then I saw one last one by my feet. I think I was already carrying other things and almost couldn't be bothered putting them down to pick it up. But I did, and I had that sixth sense of a feeling that this was special. When it came back cut

and polished from Robin it had quite a small face –
the blue-grey colour of a cat's fur I described before
– with the rings shaped like a kite. I've thought of
it as the Kite ever since: my treasure of a memory.

Where We Come From

Far down farm tracks and the edges of forest
are the sepia memories of the photographs that
*   inhabit us;*
from rivers where we swam in childhood
where we were not allowed after ten o'clock
on summer nights when the sky went yellow
and there was nothing but insects and the
*   flickering of bats.*
We come from stories and there are whole
*   unwritten books about us*
lying in the library of our hearts;
and we spend the rest of our lives
finding the right road back to read them.

The Santa Crux Well

I've always had a fascination for wells. Perhaps the first one I knew was in *Moonfleet*, when there's a descent into the darkness of a well in a basket in the hunt for the diamond. The next well I knew and came to love was the one shaped by the words of Seamus Heaney. But those I've encountered in reality have not been the classic fairy tale wells, neat stone ones with buckets, where you peer far down and play wonderful games with the echoes, watching the reflection of your face dark and rippled. Instead, what I've known far more have been springs, unadorned in the middle of moorland, surrounded by granite boulders and all but impossible to find if you hadn't first known where they were.

I've come over time to love these springs, having seen enough of the Scottish castle wells that tend to be smelly, with a glittering of coins on the bottom however many feet below. Those wells have come to feel dull and military; they've grown stale and dry after however many centuries of disuse. But

the truly ancient ones – the springs on the moorland – go on sparkling and dancing with a pure
water that reaches the soul when you drink it.
Sometimes they're marked on the map but they can
take long enough to find because there's little to
show for them when you get there. And I think to
myself: just how long have they been known? For
what could be more magical than a pure bubbling
silver of water appearing from the dark peat? Little
wonder our ancestors thought such places holy and
made pilgrimages to them around the first of May
when the old first day of summer fell. Little wonder
too they believed the water would heal whooping
cough, foot sores, stomach troubles and whatever
else besides.

I've long wanted to work with a scientist on a book
about Scottish springs: taking water from each one to
work out the minerals held by that particular spring,
then considering the specific ailments the people had
believed would be healed by it. Who's to say they
weren't sometimes right and it wasn't just superstition? But perhaps too it was just as much the benefit
of perfectly pure spring water compared to what they
drank every day. Maybe it was a bit of both.

I first became fascinated by the stories of wells
and springs when I came to live in Dunkeld at the
heart of Highland Perthshire. It must have been

after being lent old maps and books, for I remember reading several that had to do with the Cathedral and the village. But then I found another map that showed the surrounding area lying behind Dunkeld; a moorland plateau with its lochs and ancient tracks. I came to find a part above the hamlet of Butterstone that was criss-crossed by ancient paths, marked with early settlements and hut circles.

There in the middle of it all was marked something in Gothic script: the Santa Crux Well. This was long before the internet so I wrote the name down and didn't even know for sure how it was to be pronounced – it was later I learned it sounded like some city in the southern states of America. Those were the days when we relied on books for our research, and I started to read up on the story of the well, more and more intrigued by it and the place where it was sited. Back in those days the frustrating thing was that the books you found on a certain area or subject were sometimes valuable and sometimes verging on useless. It was akin to finding a giant horse chestnut newly fallen from the tree above and being completely sure it would contain a great shining treasure. When you opened it with trembling hands you discovered to your frustration a conker the size of a button. Sometimes the book I'd dig out, the one from which I'd hoped to glean most, would contain nothing but a couple of lines. Then the smallest and least promising of the lot would have a whole chapter on the history of the well.

What became clear was that the Santa Crux Well, up on those lonely moors, had come to be of great importance in pre-Reformation days. How early the May day pilgrimages had begun it didn't reveal and perhaps couldn't, but it did make clear they'd taken place for hundreds of years. The most detailed account revealed the pilgrimage had been for thousands, that the well's name had been known as far away as France. A chapel was built for the special services on pilgrimage days. Then all of it was ruined by drunkenness and revelry and the pilgrimages had had to end. But what if that story had been constructed because all of it was disliked and the new powers wanted it swept away? It was linked to the Roman Catholic Church, and all the clutter of perceived superstition and idolatry was being swept away by a new Protestant authority. The chapel had been destroyed.

I lived in Dunkeld for a good many years, and over that time I began to form some kind of picture, however fragmented and misty, of what the place might have been like hundreds of years before. Those old maps and books helped. I found for one thing that Dunkeld was encircled by wells and springs bearing the names of saints. For whatever reason, the Santa Crux Well was the exception: perhaps its name indicated its pre-eminence. But I came to believe that that procession, that pilgrimage to a lonely location far out in the wilds of the moorlands, must surely have put Dunkeld on the early maps. Dunkeld was thought of always as a place on the border between the relatively civilised part of Scotland and that which was not: the part wild with clansmen and wolves and roadless. Dunkeld was the edge of it all. But what came to me was that these pilgrims coming to visit the Santa Crux Well would have required hospitality and lodging. They would have been travelling with sick children and with friends, hoping that water from the well might bring healing. They would have needed places to stay in Dunkeld before and after the day of the pilgrimage. But that was all possible: the monks of Dunkeld Cathedral had had an infirmary so taking care of the sick would have been a central part of their mission. There must have been places to stay and people to care for them.

I'll never forget the first time I went to visit the well. It was a morning in springtime; it can't have been many days on one or other side from the first of May. I walked beside woodland loud with the shrieking of jays and saw the dark flashes of their flight ahead of me. I came to lochans lying impossibly blue under the spring breeze. It was a landscape where I could imagine wildcats, then and now. I climbed and climbed but not steeply, so that when I stopped at last and turned, I realised I was looking a long way down to smudged grey lowlands. But I didn't meet a single living soul; I walked the track in complete quiet until I came to the hillock where I reckoned the chapel must have stood.

It took quite a time for me to find the well itself. As with other moorland springs there was little to reveal its location. It was unobtrusive, timeless, hidden: nothing more than a deep hollow with a pool, and there under the surface of the water, deep down, was a font. I remember it being light and made perhaps of terracotta. My guess is that it had survived for hundreds of years and had been brought most likely from the chapel on the hill after it had been destroyed. It was the last remnant of the pre-Reformation story, that ancient pilgrimage. Of course I had to drink from the water: it was clear and pure and lovely, and somehow it reached a very deep place.

Back in those days I was very involved with Dunkeld Cathedral and its activities. I was supremely aware as a person of faith that there were other denominations in Dunkeld: the Episcopalians and Catholics first and foremost. There wasn't a great deal done to bring us together: we had our separate services and we operated in our different worlds. I thought of how special it would be if we could join together on the first Sunday of May each year and walk back along the miles of track to the Santa Crux Well. It would be an act in itself but it would be symbolic too, not least after the hurt of the Reformation. It would be a putting aside of all the petty things that divided us and a simple but profound re-enactment of the journey of faith that united us. For there are wells at the heart of the Old and New Testament alike. That pilgrimage hasn't happened yet but I dare to hope it might. And that it might bring a kind of healing; not the kind we imagined would come from drinking water we once thought held a kind of magic, some special power, but another kind of healing and one that lasts.

At Last

It was then that morning
he saw and understood
what it meant, what all this meant;
to be caught here in a place of brokenness —
the rubble of the rocks, the useless lochans,
the unarable land, the relentless days
when there was no going out, no respite;
that it was about this, the wonder of all this,
taking the whole heart hostage.

The Oaks

For a good while, a number of years, I laid it all to one side. I remembered Alastair's oaks, but as little more than a fascinating story. What must have brought it all back to prominence in my mind was working with my wife, Kristina, on the Celtic Christian retreats we lead on Iona. We were digging ourselves into that early Celtic world and all its practices and beliefs to explore the deepest roots. Inevitably we began thinking about oaks: how they had been sacred to the Celts and to the Druids before them; how so many places in Ireland and Scotland had been given names from the Irish-Gaelic word for 'oak'; how those oaks had been used by the Celts as sacred groves; and how their galls had been ground down for making ink for writing. What came back to me then was what Alastair had written about in his piece for my book *Iona: The Other Island* – that perhaps the cluster of stunted oaks he had stumbled over went right back to those first days when Columba came with his twelve followers to Iona.

There aren't many trees on the island. The few that do grow are to be found in the village, up round what is now the Heritage Centre: large, mature sycamores. It's the one place on the island it's possible for a moment to feel in a wood and back on mainland Scotland. Otherwise there are no trees, as Iona is composed of moor and rugged granite outcrops, with the middle belt of the island being more fertile; rough grazing for sheep and meadows. But there are no trees. There's heather and occasional stunted bushes that have been sculpted by the wind, but nothing more. There are no trees whatsoever in the southern part of Iona where Alastair said he'd found them, and that was why his oaks intrigued me so much and why I yearned to find them, to know he hadn't dreamed them but that they were real.

I did realise that might never happen. Strange that an island three miles in length and just one and a half in width should be able to hide so much, yet it does. After all these years of visiting and exploring, there are still parts I don't truly know. Especially in the more rugged parts of the south-east and south-west where at times the walking verges on dangerous. There are little coves I haven't found and shoulders of hills I just can't reach. Part of me is glad and wants to keep it that way; part of me is frustrated. But I know I'll die not knowing the whole island.

The Oaks

It was the great Scottish environmentalist and writer Alastair McIntosh who first set me off on a search I hope now will become a pilgrimage, if not every year then as often as possible. I was working on another book, an account of some of the many hidden corners of the island of Iona so many pilgrims know nothing about. The sad truth is that when they visit in high summer they've time only to see what I call the Vatican City of Iona (the Abbey, St Oran's Chapel and the Nunnery) before they have to hurry back to get the ferry. For me they've missed out on the spiritual richness of so many other places: the tiny coves, the secret glens, the ancient wells. I asked a few friends with strong connections to Iona to add chapters on those places most special to them, and one of those I asked was Alastair. It was no surprise that Alastair came back to me in due time with the most extraordinary piece of writing about stunted oaks he had discovered once near the Marble Quarry. In the piece of writing he'd produced were references to Syria, to Columba and to Gaelic. All that should have come as little surprise: I see Alastair as a kind of excited puppy; a thinker and writer who scurries about exploring and digging through all manner of cultures and stories, bringing back always the most extraordinary set of clues you could imagine.

I was most intrigued by his stunted oaks, and when next I met him I asked at once if he really couldn't remember exactly where he'd seen them. His answer served only to madden me the more: 'Oh, perhaps I dreamed the whole thing!' I got no more from him than that, but it left me wanting only to prove him wrong.

That part of Iona is particularly difficult to navigate, and the Marble Quarry notoriously hard to find. My own sister Helen was once leading the weekly pilgrimage from the Abbey: at that time she was Peace and Justice Worker for the Iona Community. Helen, who'd led the first Scottish women's climbing expedition to Greenland, where they'd done some first ascents, failed to find the Marble Quarry. They tramped disconsolately round the south-east corner of the island for a while, most likely in the wind and the drizzle, until Helen admitted defeat.

That part of the island is also very cliffy; not only is it complicated and confusing trying to find your way about, it can also be dangerous. I have been there myself, looking for one of the other little coves in that south-east corner, and given up because I realised I was in danger of falling, and that if I did, I might not be found for a fair old time. It's both wild and remote.

The Oaks

I think I'd rather realised it wasn't likely I'd find Alastair's oaks. For one thing I didn't relish spending hours searching in vain for them down at the Marble Quarry. From childhood days it's never been a place I've wanted to explore or even wanted to be. It represents an important enough chapter in Iona's story: how the marble was extracted and taken off to be carved and polished into numerous beautiful decorative pieces. But the empty eyes of the abandoned workers' cottages and the rusting machinery, much as they may be interesting as part of that story, don't resonate with me all the same. I can't say more than that.

Then I shared the story of the oaks with our retreatants. It was now a part of our account of the Celtic Christian homage of oaks. And late one afternoon, Alan and Peter, two of our group, came back to the Argyll Hotel brimming with excitement and with pictures to show me, because they had managed to discover the oaks. They had found this sacred grove of strong oaks, leaves all rusting in the autumn, real, with Alastair having been right after all.

This is the pilgrimage that I still have to make and that I want to make as long as I'm strong enough to do it. I want to go in the autumn to collect acorns from those oaks and bring them back to send away as gifts for Christmas. An acorn from Iona, and more than likely from a grove of oaks that was planted all those centuries ago by Columba and his followers; oaks that have survived the storms of fifteen hundred years. What more exciting gift could there be?

Awakening

Out of twelve acorns I picked in the wood
just one grew tall. I'd been away
the first half of July, came back
to thunder, floods, a garden gone to seed.
And then, that evening, I saw the stem
rising high as my hand.
I bent to behold a miracle,
the bitterness of weeds and grass all gone.
I touched three leaves – crinkled things
with cut-out edges, like those of grown-up oaks.
Eleven acorns still lay fast asleep
deep in dark earth. One had become a tree.

The Northern Lights

The best winter I've ever known was in Arctic Norway. I grew up with dreichness: the cold, damp windiness of Octobers and Novembers that often seemed to trail on far longer than their thirty days. I was born at the end of November and through my childhood I don't remember once seeing the sun on my birthday. Instead that dreichness persisted, and often it trudged on into the spring: days that grew half-dark by half past three in the afternoon. And then, after the even damper and gloomier winters at university in Glasgow, doubtless made worse by the dirty skies, I went to Arctic Norway.

I travelled by train from Trondheim to almost the last station on the line and a place called Rognan. I was staying where Norway was at its thinnest, and by the time I got out in the township where I'd stay for a full academic year I was fifty miles north of the Arctic Circle. When I arrived in that corner of Nordland it was autumn: crisp and bright and made of pine trees and the scent of resin.

I was reminded all the time of Strathspey – the area around the Cairngorm mountains – with its long wolves of hills and deep woodlands. The hills of northern Norway are much more akin to those in Scotland; they're not the jagged peaks we associate with the fjord country of the west, but older and more worn summits. Then, out of nowhere one morning in the absolute quiet, the snow began falling; flakes that flickered against the needles of the pines. I went to a window to watch that snow and sat there like a child, mesmerised, as still it fell until the cars outside the college became strange shapes and the trees held armfuls of heavy white. Six whole feet of snow. I remember sitting at the window of my room watching the train burning north that night from Trondheim, a glow-worm of twelve carriages clattering on into the darkness.

Then came *mørketiden* – the time of darkness – however many weeks of sunlessless. I won't pretend I didn't struggle with that dark because I believe now you have to grow up with such weeks of winter dark to become used to it. And there are plenty of northern Norwegians who struggle with it themselves; they travel south each winter to find light. To go outside at noon into what I came to call moon and stars darkness is strange and eerie;

it takes time to grow used to the total absence of the sun. I realised my mind was beginning to play tricks on me when I sat one afternoon in my room and began thinking that if I were to dig into the roof space I might find the sun. So I won't pretend I didn't struggle with the dark, but there were things that made it bearable in the end. They made it not just bearable; somehow they even rendered it wonderful.

The first thing that happened was that it froze: a full thirty degrees Centigrade (more than twenty degrees Fahrenheit below freezing). I'd known frost in my childhood in Scotland, of course. In a severe winter in the midst of the dreichness we might have a few nights when the temperature would sink to ten or twelve degrees Centigrade below zero, and to my delight I'd be able to make a slide. But this was much colder. This was something else.

The strange thing was that seldom did you feel the full severity of that frost. I'm reminded of the cold in Jack London's *To Build a Fire:* you only feel it truly when you're wet and the wind blows. Just once or twice I was out in the township of Rognan and felt the wind against my face. It wasn't even the full wind; just a breeze, but it was enough to make you want to cry. Then the cold hurt badly.

But what the frost did was diminish the darkness. A glitter came to the six feet of snow; everywhere you went it danced with light. Everywhere were great crystals of frost. And the other gift we received was that of the Northern Lights.

I would go out onto the balcony outside our boarding house to watch them rise, each and every night. I've never known a bigger silence than the one that winter. The college buildings were all made of wood and were scattered through the pine forest. Our little boarding house stood on the edge of it all, with a clear view of the whole northern sky. The magical thing was that you never knew for sure what colours we'd be given: blues and greens for sure, but only occasionally reds.

The lights would grow like great mouths and then shrink again. At times the sky would become a kind of firework display as great silver columns rose from behind the mountains. But this was a firework display in slow motion: you watched it all change in the same way you'd imagine seeing faces speaking, but silently and syllable by syllable. Sometimes it seemed that on the nights they were particularly bright there was a strange crackling in the pine trees around us. I've heard and read of it since. It is a kind of static that comes with the Northern Lights. There would be others out on balconies close by and further off. I remember one woman telling me there were superstitions associated with the lights that were remembered still. If you whistled to them or waved a handkerchief they would grow in strength.

Of course the Sami people had their own legends about how the Northern Lights came to be. I thought of them in the end as the ghosts of strange horses, for with a little imagination that's what they resembled. They weren't separate shades of light; they flowed together and became like creatures, but for me they were the memory of what once had been, left dancing for ever in the winter skies.

I had seen the Northern Lights now and again in Scotland in my childhood, but never like this. Usually they're just a vague green glow in the northern skies, something you dare hope might be the real thing. But once I was camping with a friend in the Perthshire hills. The night skies were perfectly bright: a beautiful blue that went on deepening as it neared midnight. Suddenly there were lights all around us, as though strange torch beams played hide and seek with us, and for a time we chased about, trying to work out who might be there and why they were playing tricks on us. It was only much later I read of similar sightings in

the Scottish hills and worked out that it must have
been the Northern Lights.

My wife, Kristina, is from the south of Sweden;
all her life she's wanted to experience the magic
of what in Scotland have been called the Merry
Dancers. But we were in Arctic Norway and
Arctic Finland together at the wrong time of year:
there was little hope of them. Then this winter,
at the end of an unusually clear few days of cold,
she came into the sitting room to find me. I was
coming to the end of a phone conversation but
she was quite calm and didn't hurry me. When
I'd finished she told me she thought the Northern
Lights might be up.

We went out together into the cold brilliance of
the night and stood beyond the back door, looking
right up into the northern skies. We've wonderful
clarity in the skies above our island; there are no
street lights to cloud the night. We waited, watching, and inevitably I felt back in Arctic Norway,
wondering what colours we might be given this
night, now just a beautiful pale glowing that came
and went in organ pipes above the low, low hills.
A ghostly white and green, and perhaps a hint
of red there sometimes too. But it was them, it
was the lights, and my heart was glad for Kristina,
for she was seeing them at last. This shortest of

pilgrimages, to just beyond the back door. We'll make it again in the winters to come, doubtless, not knowing if we'll be rewarded with lights or not. But for me the pilgrimage is not about the certainty of finding, it's about making the journey – whether short or long – and about all that's found in that journey. It's about what you carry back with you, and that may not be what you set out first to find.

Of Price and Worth

Let the ordinary be in your hand;
hold it open and imagine a bird landing,
offering all it possesses in trust
 to come to you.

Learn to look for the little things
that weigh nothing at all,
 but fill the heart with such light
they can never be measured.

Kenneth Steven is a widely published Scottish poet, novelist, essayist and translator who discovered his love for the natural world during his childhood; a reverence for the wonder of words soon followed. His writing, inspired mainly by the wild landscapes of the Highlands, has won many awards. His BBC radio documentary on the remote Atlantic island of St Kilda won a prestigious Sony Award, and he has written and narrated several series of the BBC Radio 3 *Essays* programme.